Vision Marksmanship

Vision Marksmanship®

A Model for Personal and Organizational Success

How To Stay On Track To Achieve Your Vision

Steven Mitchell

Paperback ISBN: 9798376524947

Copyright © 2023 by Steven P. Mitchell.

All rights reserved.

Vision Marksmanship®

Model for Personal and Organizational Success

STAYING ON TRACK TO ACHIEVE VISION

#Strategic Planning

#Action Planning

#Project Management

#Goal Setting

#Vision Achievement

#Leadership

#Career Coaching

Vision Marksmanship ® is a registered trademark by Steven P. Mitchell.

Table of Contents

Learning Objectives	viii
Introduction	1
MVGVP	5
Vision Marksmanship® Leadership	13
Strategic Planning	17
Action Plan Development	23
Barriers to Achievement	31
Staying on Track	35
Team Care	41
Summary	43

LEARNING OBJECTIVES

Section 1 – Introduction

- Introduction to Vision Marksmanship ®
- Introduction to MVGVP

Section 2 – MVGVP

- The reader will be introduced to Mission, Vision, Goals, Values and Priorities
- The reader will learn the Seven-part process to carry your MVGVP through the Planning and Vision Period.

Section 3 – Vision Marksmanship® Leadership

- The reader will become familiar with the Marksmanship of achieving a Vision.
- The reader will review Leadership Actions and Injects during Strategic Plan and Vision Achievement processes.

Section 4 - Strategic Plan

- The reader will become familiar with the basics of the strategic planning process.

Section 5 – Action Plan Development

- The reader will learn the elements of the Vision Marksmanship® Action Plan.
- The reader will be introduced to the use of SMART Goals in Action Plans.
- The reader will learn the process of turning a Vision and Strategic Plan into a detailed Action Plan for the Organization, Division and Team Levels.

Section 6 – Barriers to Achievement

- The reader will become familiar with the various Barriers to Goal Achievement.
- The reader will learn ways to overcome Barriers to Achievement.

Section 7 – Staying on Track

- The reader will become familiar with the Leadership tasks and activities necessary to keep the various processes on track toward the desired Vision Achievement.

Section 8 – Team Care

- The reader will learn the importance of Team Care techniques during both Mission and Vision Achievement processes.

SECTION 1 – INTRODUCTION

Effective Leaders create a Vision, and then move the organization or group forward to achieve the Vision. Whether you are in the Private Sector, Public Sector, or a Non-Profit you have an idea or Vision where you would like the organization to move toward. Every organization is busy day to day putting out a product or service. Most organizations are lean placing more emphasis of day-to-day issues on the leaders. The leaders spend so much of the time during the day on operational issues, putting out fires, and handling what walks in the door, the VISION is forgotten. The organization operates and churns out a product or service, but there is no movement forward, no improvement. The organization simply revolves in circles. The organization gets off track, off target due to the lack of marksmanship to keep the Vision on target. Vision Marksmanship®, if used correctly and wisely, establishes an Organization Vision, and keeps the organization on track toward that Vision while accomplishing the day-to-day Mission. The Vision Marksmanship® model allows all levels within an organization to learn and practice methods to move toward a Vision while still maintaining the Mission and day to day operations.

Vision is not simply for the organization as a whole, but also for Divisions, Work Units and Project Teams. The Vision for these sub-units must be in alignment with the overall Organization Vision, however the creation of such a Team Vision will help the Team stay on track by using Vision Marksmanship.

What you'll learn

- ✓ You will learn about a program that can help any organization achieve a desired Vision for organizational success.

- ✓ You will understand how the Vision Marksmanship Model will keep your organization on track with the ability to accomplish a strategic plan.

- ✓ You will learn the difference between Mission and Vision, and the importance of Mission, Vision, Goals, Values and Priorities.

- ✓ At the end of the program, both Leaders and Team Members will have an understanding of the Vision Marksmanship Action Planning process.

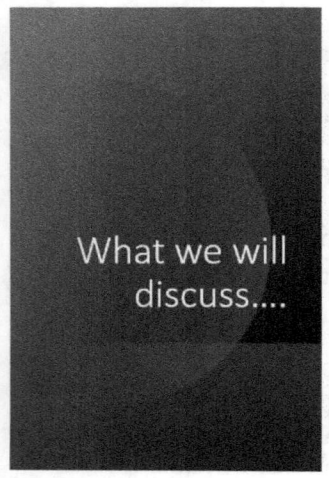
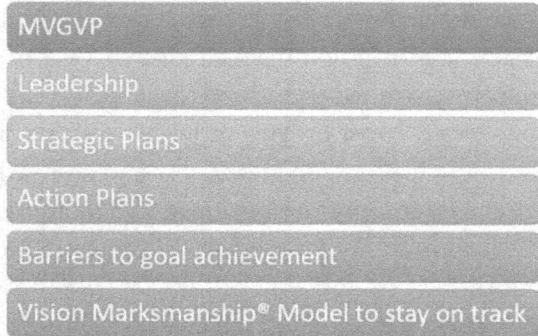

Vision Marksmanship® is a program that can be used to keep the ship moving in the right direction, toward the desired Vision. The Vision Marksmanship® program typically starts after the Vision creation and Strategic Plan development acting as the Action plan, or part of the action plan.

Vision Marksmanship® is an exclusive program designed to help organizations succeed in achieving the Organization Vision, and help human talent move toward their own personal professional Vision. It is a road map to success. Marksmanship is the skill of keeping on target. In our case we are referring to keeping an organization as a whole, or a work unit or project team, on target toward achieving a specific Vision, Goal or set of Goals.

VISION MARKSMANSHIP FOCUSES ON THE FOLLOWING AREAS TO KEEP THE ORGANIZATION MOVING FORWARD TO THE VISION

Mission   Vision   Goals

- Leadership
- Decision Making
- Budget
- Goal Alignment
- Action Plans
- Barriers
- Course Correction

Values   Priorities

Vision Marksmanship

SECTION 2 – MVGVP

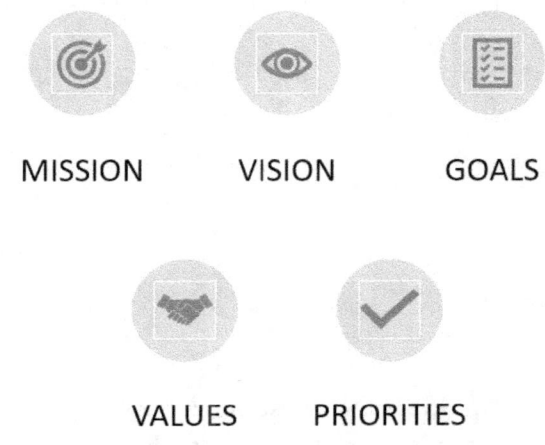

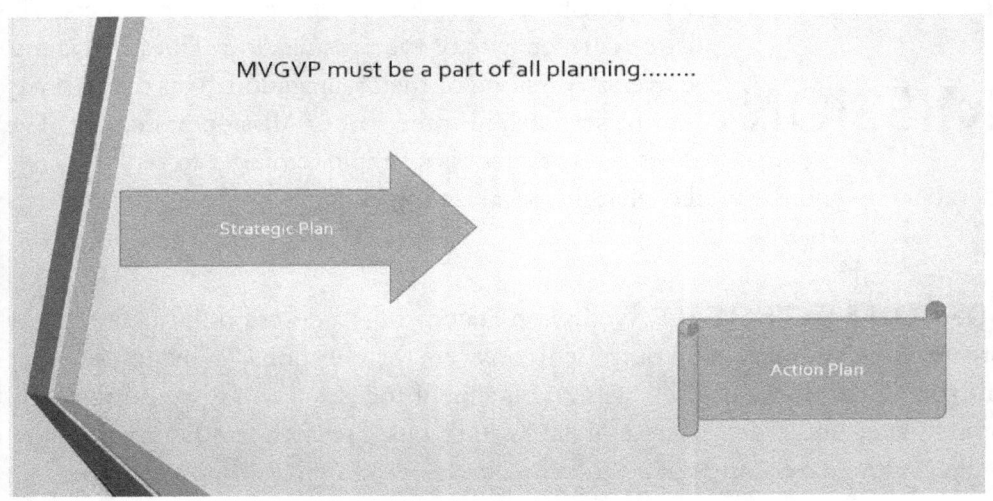

The discovery and development of the MVGVP must occur at the beginning. Once determined and developed, the MVGVP must be carried through all planning phases.

MISSION vs VISION

Let's explore the difference of answering the questions "What do we do?" and "Why do we exist?" compared to "What will we look like in five years?"

MISSION

MISSION. Most organizations provide a particular service or product to an identified set of customers or clients. Day to day operations is established to accomplish these services or deliver these products. This is the current state of the organization. Thus, this is the current "Mission" of the organization. This may or may not be set forth in some sort of Mission Statement. The Mission Statement is a simple reminder to the membership and the public what the organization currently is set-up to provide.

MISSION STATEMENT. A Mission Statement is a description of an organization's fundamental purpose. It answers the questions "Why do we exist?" and/or "What do we do?" A Mission Statement focuses on an organization's present state and articulates the organization's purpose both for those within the organization and for the public and customers.

VISION

VISION. A Vision is a picture of the organization at some point in the future. It is recommended that point be within a definite time frame, but not always the case. While it is important for the organization to concentrate on the daily operations of the Mission, it is equally as important that the organization complete tasks, goals, and objectives toward the Vision as well. Typically, the Mission will take up the majority of an organization's time. However, it is important that time is set aside for Vision achievement as well.

VISION STATEMENT

A Vision Statement is a picture of your organization in the future, but it is also so much more. It is your inspiration, the framework for all of your strategic planning. A Vision may apply to an entire organization or to a single division or unit. A Vision Statement answers the question "Where do we want to go?" A Vision statement reminds you of what you are trying to build and focuses on an organization's future state.

Answering these questions gives you a Vision

- What does your professional life look like five years from now?
- What does the business you own look like five years from now?
- What does the business you manage look like five years from now?
- What does your public sector department look like five years from now?
- What does your not-for-profit organization look like five years from now?
- What does your work team look like five years from now?

A Goal is an end point toward which effort has been directed. SMART Goals are an important part of the Vision Marksmanship® Action Planning process.

Specific * Measurable* Attainable* Realistic* Time Specific

GOALS

Values in an organization are a set of ideals that are important to the organization and the Human Talent within the organization. Successful organizations typically adopt, instill, and reinforce a set of Core Values. These values are utilized in everything from hiring, to motivation, Vision achievement and even performance correction.

VALUES

Priorities are items, goals and objectives established by order of importance or urgency. For example, in a 5-year strategic plan it may not be possible or feasible to attempt the completion of all facets of the plan at one time. Annual, monthly, weekly, and even at times daily priorities must be established.

PRIORITIES

> **Note**
>
> Day to day Mission operations and actions moving toward a Vision can and should co-exist. Use Vision Marksmanship to make sure that both stay on track.

Some organizations create and use Vision Statements that may be flashy or sound great to the Public, but either are not grounded in future reality or the organization has already been at the point of the Vision for some time. Your Vision Statement should actually clarify the actual realistic Vision at some point in the future.

- What challenges do we have now or expect in the Vision period?
- What changes do we expect in our community?
- What problems or challenges do we intend to solve?
- Where do we expect the organization to go?
- What do we expect the organization to look like or strive for?
- What services that may be different do we expect to offer?
- What key words describe what we will look like?
- What modern practices have been or will be updated or improved?

Vision Marksmanship

Organization Vision and Goal Alignment

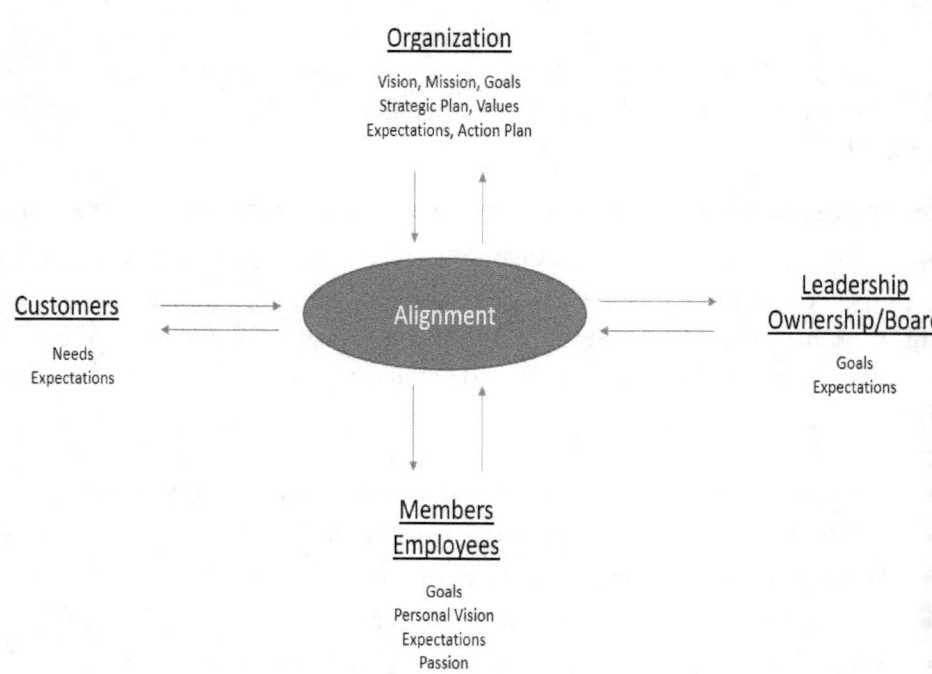

Seven-part process to carry your MVGVP through the Planning and Vision Period

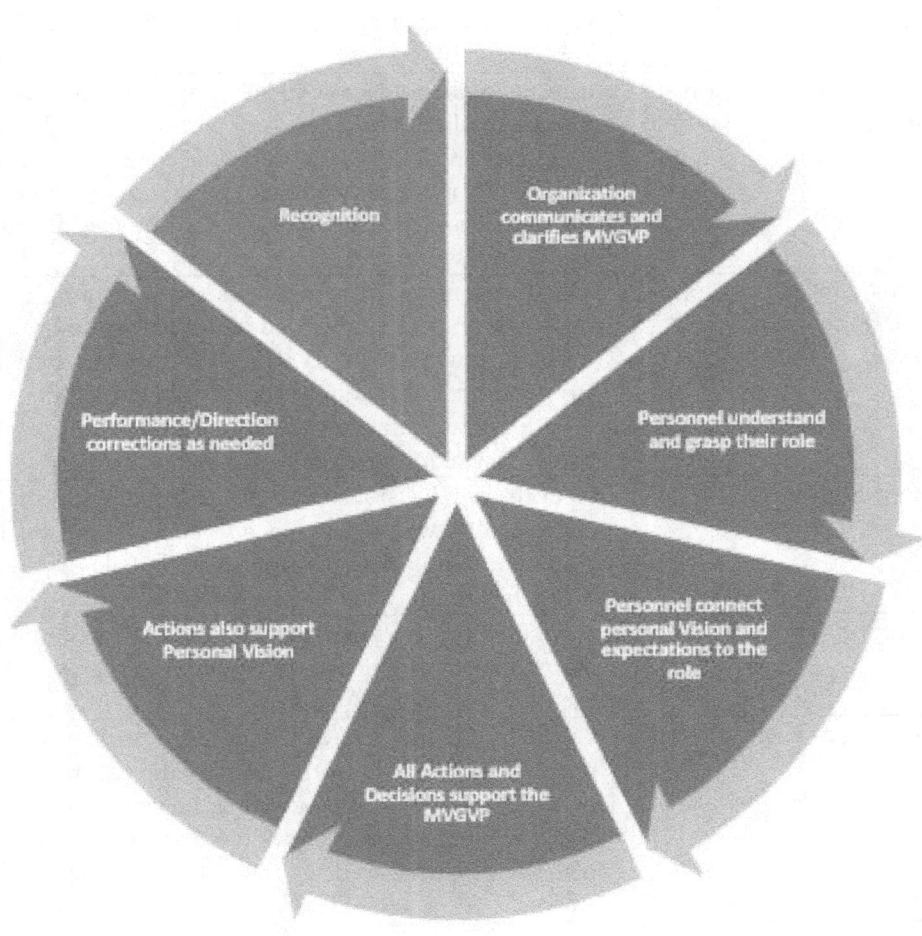

Clarify and Communicate MVGVP	Leadership at all levels must have the ability to clarify and communicate the MVGVP. This must not only occur at the beginning of the process but must continue throughout the project or Vision period. Leadership must be able to link the MVGVP to daily operations.
Stakeholders must understand role	Internal Stakeholders at all levels must understand what exactly their role is within the MVGVP and Strategic Plan.
Vision and Expectation Alignment	Internal Stakeholders at all levels at all levels must be able to align personal Vision and Goals with the organization MVGVP. This is vital to organization success. Properly aligned goals can help a person move forward in an organization as the organization itself moves forward.
Actions/Decisions support MVGVP	The decision-making process used at all operational, supervisory, management and administrative levels must support the MVGVP. This includes everything from a normal day to day operational line/staff question with quick decisions to more complicated issues that require research and study.
Actions Support Personal Vision	Actions and decisions made by leadership and the team should, when possible, also support and be in alignment with personal professional goals of those on the team.
Corrections as Needed	Direction and Performance corrections can come in many forms but are crucial to staying on target to the ultimate desired Vision.
Recognition/Evaluation	Evaluation of the strategic plan, process or project must be ongoing on both a formal and informal basis. Day to day corrections can be made to stay on track, while more formal evaluations and correction plans can be used to drive toward the targeted Vision.

Section 3 - VISION MARKSMANSHIP® LEADERSHIP

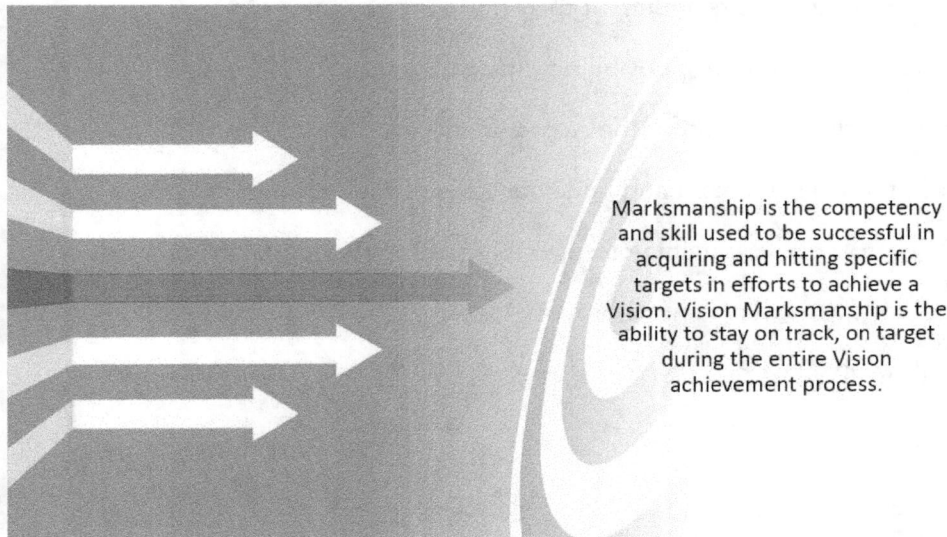

Marksmanship is the competency and skill used to be successful in acquiring and hitting specific targets in efforts to achieve a Vision. Vision Marksmanship is the ability to stay on track, on target during the entire Vision achievement process.

Leadership within an organization comes in many forms. It may be formal or informal. It is very important to organizational success that Leadership at all levels grasp the MVGVP. Leadership at each level to include Executive, Administrative, Managerial, Supervisorial, Team Leader and so on make decisions daily that affect the organization. Therefore, at each and every level, such decisions must support the MVGVP and the Vision process. The decision makers must ask the question "How does this decision affect the future of the organization?"

Making a decision that drives a goal or project off course can be detrimental, however may be needed from time to time based on an operational need. It is important to clarify the decision both up and down, and then develop a plan that will help bring it back in alignment with the Vision process at some point.

Vision Marksmanship

Leadership Actions:

✓ Provide clear understanding of the priorities

✓ Take daily Mission responsibilities into account

✓ Provide clear direction of the Action Plan

✓ Seek mutual agreement and understanding of the Action Plan

✓ Delegate while maintaining responsibility through accountability

✓ Do not overload personnel or work teams

✓ Follow-up

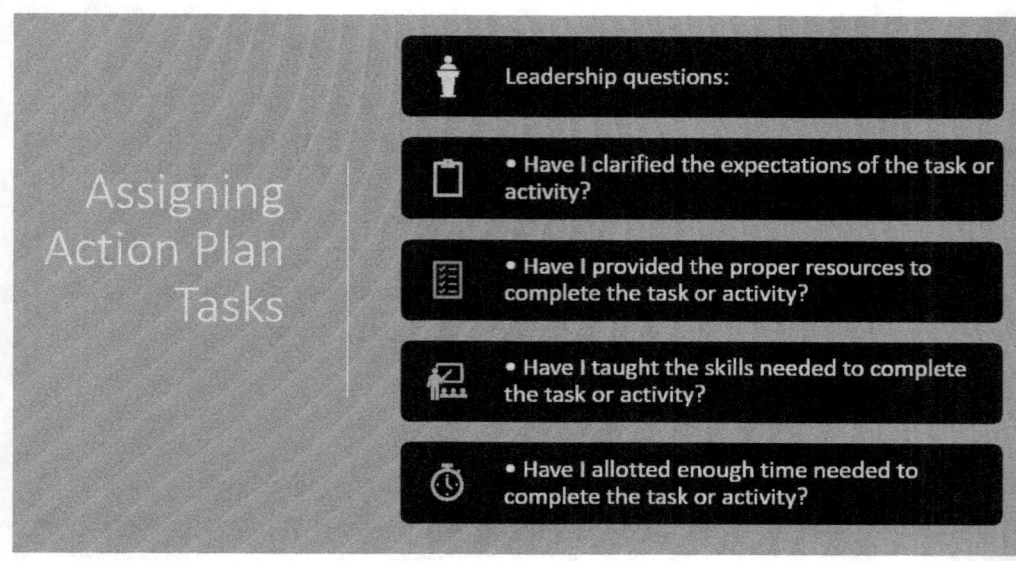

Vision Marksmanship

Below we take a look at the Strategic Planning Process as it relates to Leadership.

- After the MVGVP and Strategic Plan are finalized and agreed to, begin to Clarify and Communicate the MVGVP and the Plan.
- Once the Strategic Plan is turned into a Vision Marksmanship Action Plan Model, determine the budget and training needs for the organization, project teams, and individuals. Begin the training process.
- The Action Plan SMART Goals will identify the resources needed. Those resources need to be provided. There are two options, provide the resources or require the Team acquire the resources.
- Tasks and Activities are now assigned. At this time and throughout the task process the Leadership will need to provide support as needed. In order to accomplish this, the individual or team will need to keep the Leader up to date.
- The Leader will need to evaluate and review the progress informally and formally on a routine basis. Such review answering, "Where are we?" will define additional resources, course or performance corrections that may be needed.

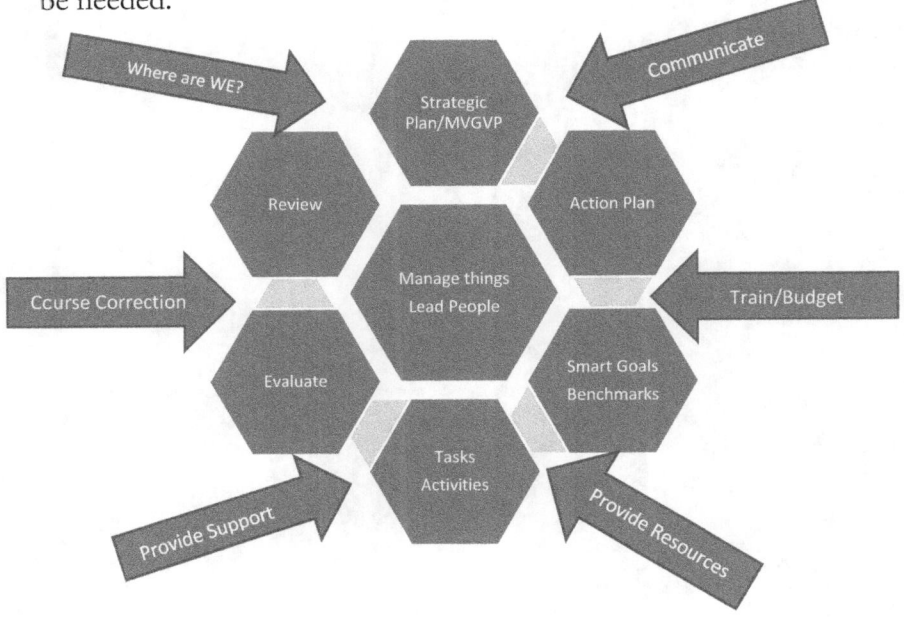

Vision Marksmanship

SECTION 4 – STRATEGIC PLANNING

Strategic Planning is the comprehensive process involving all levels of internal and external stakeholders making decisions about mid-range and long-term goals for the organization. If a Vision does not already exist, a Vision can grow out of the strategic planning process. This program will touch very briefly on Strategic Planning; however, Vision Marksmanship concentrates on the process of achieving the Vision and Goals within the Strategic Plan. If leadership is not experienced in the Strategic Planning process, bringing in a third party to assist the organization through the process may be necessary for professional results.

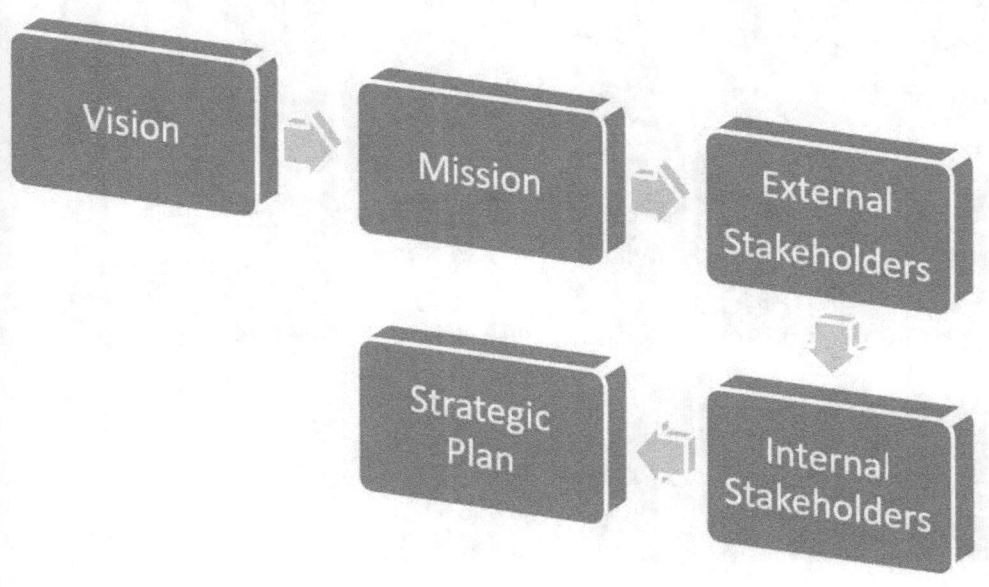

Vision Marksmanship

This graphic shows a very basic process of going from customer needs through the planning process to results. Vision Marksmanship is a detailed program that allows the organization to achieve the Vision and Strategic Plan Desired Outcomes/Goals.

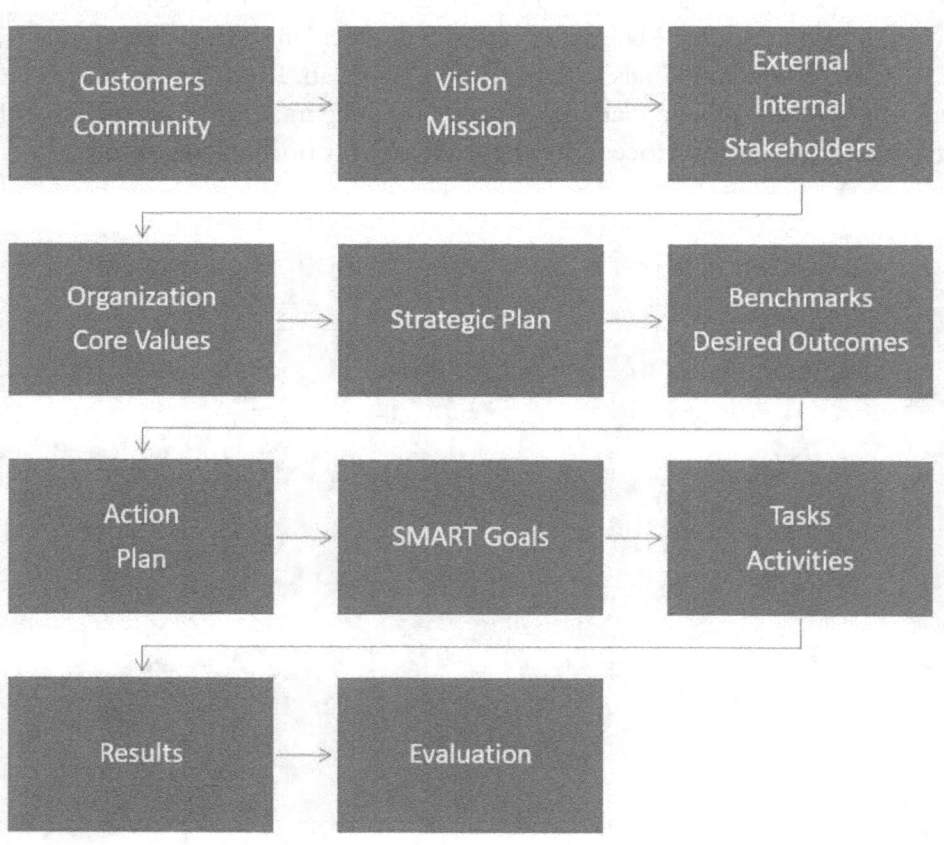

Strategic Plans typically cover a period, such as 3 to 5 years. 5-Year strategic plans are realistic to turn into action plans. An organization may also have more long-term plans as well that are a little more generic. From time to time even five-year plans may have to be altered based on internal and external factors

The final Strategic Plan will contain the Mission of the Organization, the Vision to achieve at the end of the Plan, and all of the Desired Outcomes that lead toward that Vision. Vision Marksmanship Action Planning is then utilized to ensure the achievement of those Desired Outcomes.

Basic Strategic Planning Process

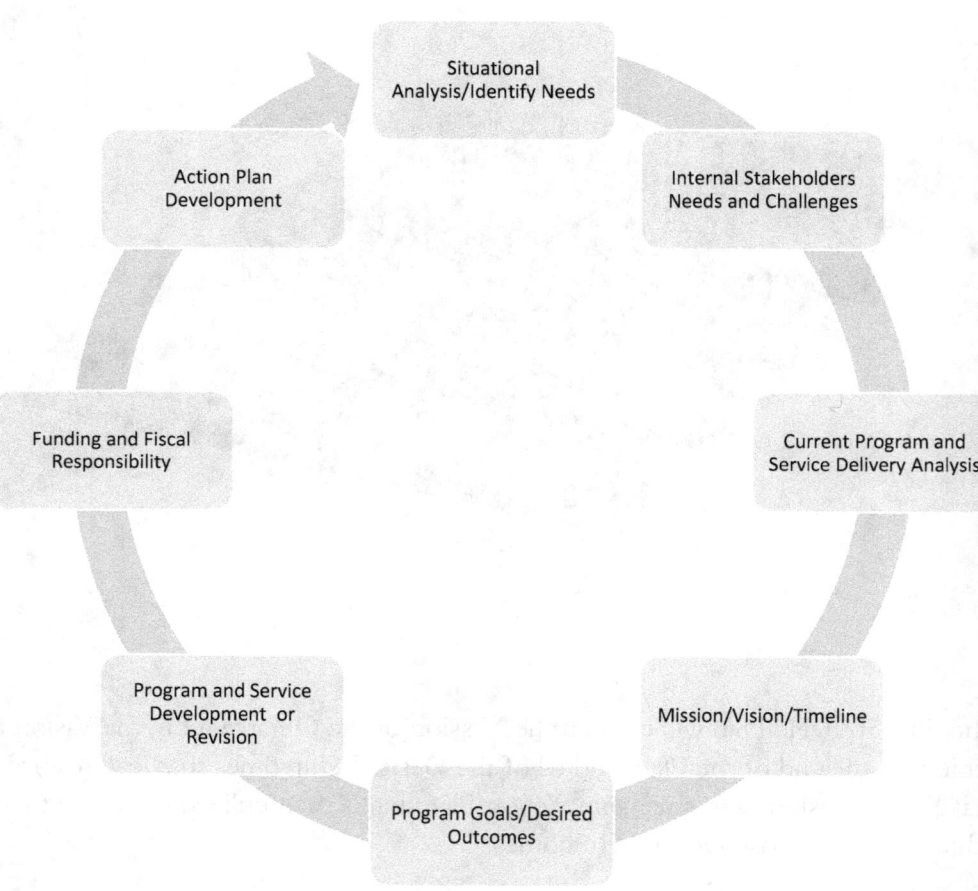

Provide for ongoing situational awareness and analysis during the planning process and throughout the Plan Period. Update as necessary.

SWOT Analysis

Consider using a SWOT analysis as part of your strategic planning process. Use individual or group sessions to help identify Strengths, Weakness, Opportunities and Threats. Consider "Threats" as the first opportunity to identify both internal and external barriers. SWOT can also be used as you are developing a new Vision and developing the action plan. SWOT is not just for organizational planning but can be used for your personal professional development planning as well.

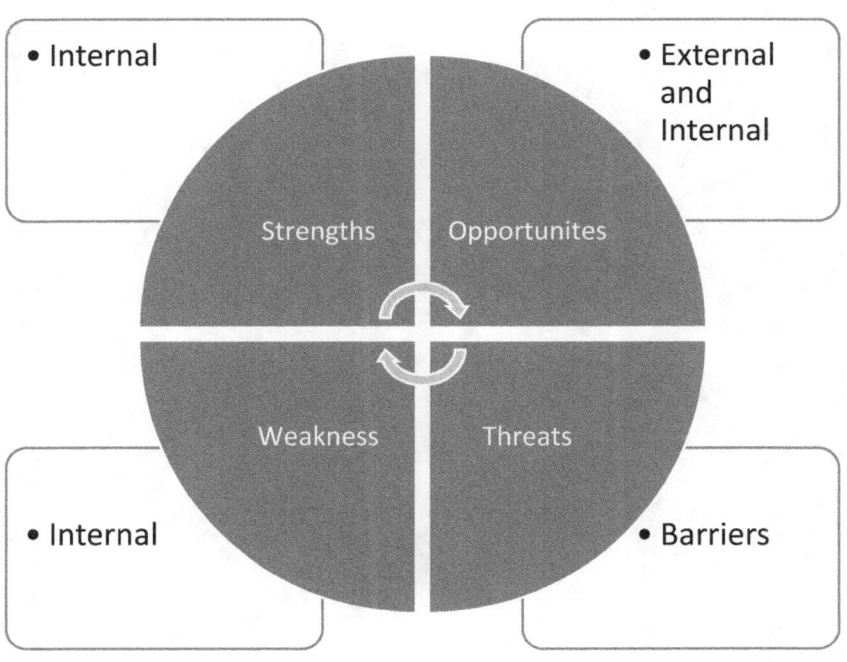

Vision Marksmanship

SECTION 5 – ACTION PLAN DEVELOPMENT

The Vision Statement, Vision Description and the Desired Outcomes that lead toward Vision Achievement should come from the Strategic Planning Process and will be part of the written Organization Strategic Plan. Breaking down the Desired Outcome Phases into Projects and SMART Goals will occur in the Action Planning Process and the written Action Plan.

VISION ACTION PLAN

- Vision Statement
- Narrative description of the Vision
- Desired Outcomes leading to Vision Achievement
- Desired Outcome Phases
- Smart Goals toward each Desired Outcome Phase

VISION ACTION PLAN ADAPTABLE

- ✓ Priorities
- Budgeting
- Resources
- Assignments
- Follow up

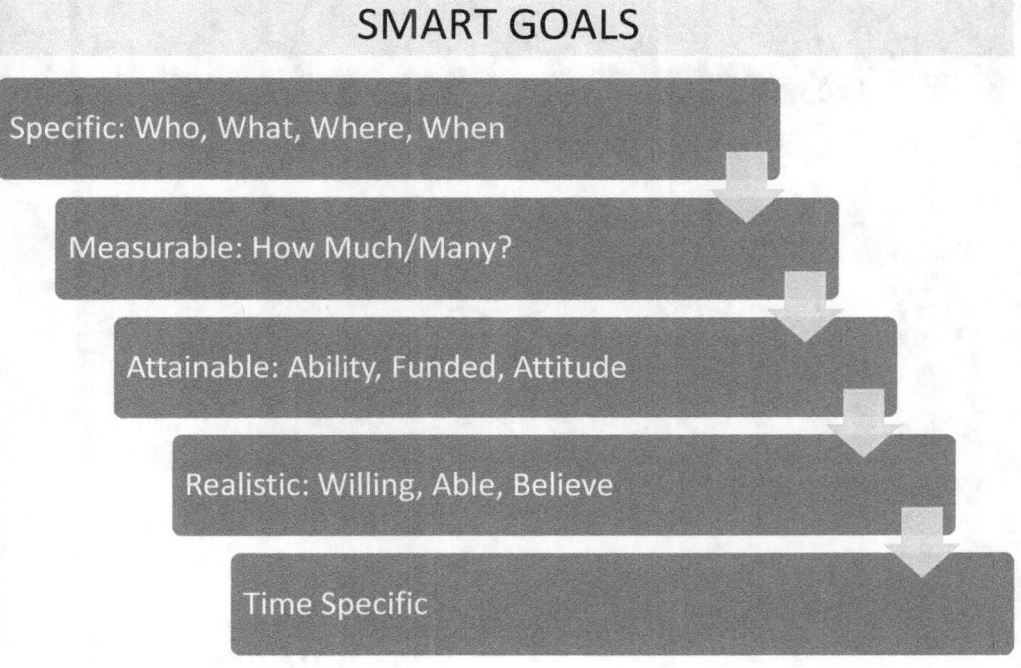

Goals are an end point toward which effort has been directed.

SMART Goals are an important part of the Vision Marksmanship Action Planning Process. They are used to break down the tasks towards each Desired Outcome. Using SMART goals will help your Action Plan stay on track.

Now we can take our first look at building the Action Plan with a Desired Outcome and a series of SMART Goals.

Desired Outcome A.

01	02	03	04
SMART Goal A-1	SMART Goal A-2	SMART Goal A-3	SMART Goal A-4

VISION

Desired Outcome A

SMART Goal A-1
SMART Goal A-2
SMART Goal A-3
SMART Goal A-4

Desired Outcome B

SMART Goal B-1
SMART Goal B-2
SMART Goal B-3
SMART Goal B-4

PRIORITIES

Priorities are items, goals or objectives established by order of importance or urgency. For example, in a 5-year strategic plan it is not possible nor efficient to attempt to complete all facets of the plan at one time. Annual, monthly, weekly, and even daily priorities must be established.

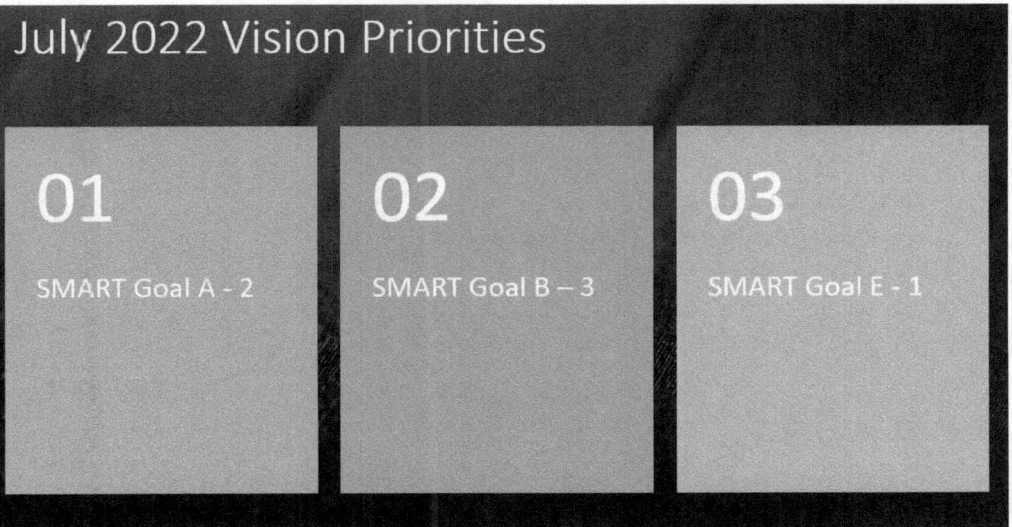

Setting the Priorities should be discussed on a regular basis during the update meetings with the individual or project team assigned to a particular Desired Outcome. There are many factors that will go into setting the current and upcoming priorities. This may include current normal operations and resulting time limits.

Action Plan Outline

Organization Level

<u>Desired Outcome A</u>

    Desired Outcome A – Phase I

    SMART GOAL A.1-1
    SMART GOAL A.1-2
    SMART GOAL A.1-3

    Desired Outcome A – Phase II

    SMART GOAL A.2-1
    SMART GOAL A.2-2
    SMART GOAL A.2-3

Division Level

<u>Desired Outcome A</u>

    Desired Outcome A – Phase I

    SMART GOAL A.1-1
- Resources Needed
- Budget Needed
- Support Needed
- Team Members Needed
- Training Required
- Assigned to
- Dates

Vision Marksmanship

Team Level

Desired Outcome A

Desired Outcome A – Phase I

SMART GOAL A.1-1

- Vison Communicated and Clarified
- Desired Outcome Communicated and Clarified
- Resources Needed
- Budget Needed
- Barriers Identified
- Support Needed/Training Provided
- Team Member Assignments
- Assignments
- Dates/Scheduling
- Support-Support-Support
- Follow up/Deal with Barriers
- Performance Course Corrections
- Recognition

Vision Marksmanship

SECTION 6 – BARRIERS TO ACHIEVEMENT

A Leader needs to be able to recognize barriers to team goal completion and be able to work with the team or individual on solutions to overcome the barrier.

Various options to barriers exist such as eliminating the barrier, overcoming the barrier, go around the barrier, plow through the barrier, or adapt to the barrier and make it work for the project. If a solution burns a bridge, you better look very carefully at the solution and determine what that does to the future of the Vision and the organization as a whole.

Some Possible Barriers to Team Goal Completion	
	Day to Day Operations, completing the Mission.
	Time was not realistic.
	Lack of proper resources.
	Inability of the Team Leader to coordinate or maintain time management.
	Lack of Team cohesiveness.
	Lack of Leadership Guidance. Loss of Focus.
	Lack of training or resources for team members.
	The Goal was not clear or not a true SMART goal. Expectations were not clear.
	Perceived priority vs actual priority.
	Is the Vision still valid?

Vision Marksmanship

Barrier	Possible Issues	Possible Solutions
Day to Day Operations	Leadership may be busy with day-to-day operations and lose sight of the Vision	Daily Use of the Vision Marksmanship Action plan
Time not realistic	Leadership did not have realistic knowledge of time requirements.	Discussions with individual or team assigned the Goal or Task, prior to setting time limit and during the process
Lack of Proper Resources	Individual/Team finds the proper resources are not available to complete the goal.	Proper planning at the beginning or give the individual/team authority to acquire resources.
Coordination/Time Management Issues	The Leader has a difficult time in coordination of projects or struggles with time management.	Training Performance Correction Leader Replacement
Lack of Cohesiveness	The Team does not seem to be working together well or simply cannot get along	Team Building Proper assignments Individual replacement
Loss of focus	The Leader loses focus; thus, the team eventually loses focus.	Use Action Plan to stay on track.
Lack of Training	Training needed should be identified early in the process. Needed training may also be discovered during the process.	Identify and provide training early. Identify and provide training throughout the process.
Expectations not clear.	Typically, this means that the Goal used was not a true SMART Goal, and/or the Leader did not follow the Leadership Steps of Vision Marksmanship.	Review the goal and rewrite as needed. Follow all steps of Leadership needed to set up the individual/team for success.
Priority Perceived or real	A frequent problem is for Leadership to set forth a goal for a team, but then make decisions contrary to that priority.	All levels must be on the same page. All decisions must support MVGVP and Priorities set for a particular time period.

HANDLING A BARRIER

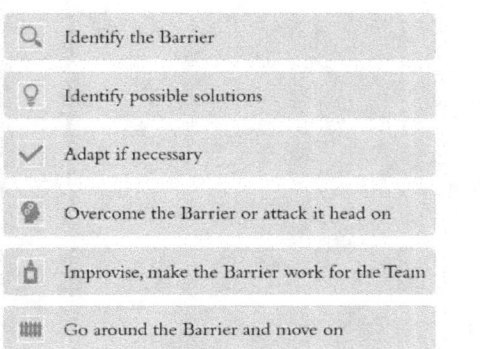

- Identify the Barrier
- Identify possible solutions
- Adapt if necessary
- Overcome the Barrier or attack it head on
- Improvise, make the Barrier work for the Team
- Go around the Barrier and move on

Note

Will attacking the barrier burn a bridge that may be needed later? What are the long and short term implications and is the result worth it?

During a 5-year strategic planning and Visioning period it is very possible for an organization to find itself in need of change due to various influences and factors, typically external. For example, the Covid Pandemic did this for many businesses. If you find the organization is off track often, or an external influence causes disruption or change, it may be time to take a look at the Vision once again. A review may find the need to change the Vision, or simply make Action Plan, Operational and timing changes to get to the original Vision as identified. It may be appropriate to bring in an outside 3rd party to assist with this review.

In order to keep the Strategic Plan, Action Plan and Visioning process on track, Leaders throughout the organization need to ask the following questions at the end of each day:

"What did WE do today to move the organization forward to the Vision?"

"What did I do today to move the organization forward to the Vision?"

It is ok if sometimes that answer is "not a thing." But if that answer starts occurring on a regular basis, it is time to step back and review priorities.

Vision Marksmanship

SECTION 7 – VISION MARKSMANSHIP STAYING ON TRACK

LEADERSHIP

- ❏ Does not micromanage
- ❏ Clarifies Expectations
- ❏ Provides Guidance and Support
- ❏ Allows the Team or Individual Assigned to accomplish the task(s)
- ❏ Tracks Progress
- ❏ Provides Performance and Course Correction
- ❏ Provides recognition

TEAM MEETINGS

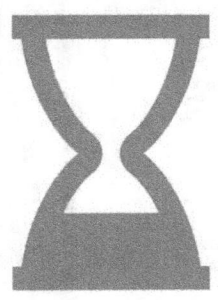

- ❏ Summary of progress
- ❏ Is your project still on track to the Desired Outcome?
- ❏ Have you run into any barriers?
- ❏ Do you need any more resources?
- ❏ Is the budget adequate?
- ❏ Is any additional training or support needed?
- ❏ Are you on time?
- ❏ Any other issues?

Vision Marksmanship

It is imperative that the Leaders at each level are on the same page at each Phase working toward a desired Vision. Everyone involved is responsible for keeping the process on track and on time, and course corrections should be allowed to be made at any level of the process to maintain focus.

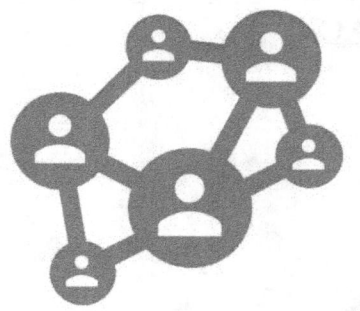

STAYING ON TRACK

Communication → Clarification → Use the Vision Marksmanship Action Planning → Commit to the Action Plan at all levels

Schedule alongside Mission/Day to Day Duties → Provide Training → Follow-up Regularly → Help Team overcome barriers

Help team with course corrections → Performance Corrections → Recognition

Day to Day Time and Task Management

Utilize a daily scheduling process that not only aids in your time management, but also will help your Visioning process stay on track while also accomplishing the day-to-day Mission. Using the ABC technique is simple and reliable. Break tasks down into this simple ABC format in order to stay within timelines. These tasks will be what you work on between other scheduled meetings, phone calls, video conferences, etc. It is important to understand that from time-to-time daily issues that come up may need to be mixed into the ABC process, slightly altering your original plan. Leave space for these injects. However, you can also use this process to help block out periods to finish important projects or tasks as needed. For example, block out half a day three days from now to accomplish something that is now in the B's. Consider using the Daily Priority Formula of Must Do 50%, Should Do 35% and Nice to Do 15%.

A = Must be accomplished today

B = Will need to be accomplished very soon, timeline closing soon.

C = Future tasks or projects that you can work on as time permits.

In our program we will also add a "P" to the process.

P = Personal Professional Development that is required, in process, to be completed soon, or desired to complete in the near future. Make sure that these at some point move into the ABCs.

Daily Task Time Management: Today's Priorities = A

- A – 1   Email/In Box
- A – 2   Daily Update
- A – 3   Must do today
- A – 4   Must do today
- A – 5   Set Next Day Priorities
- A – 6   What did we do today toward Vision Achievement?

Daily Task Time Management: Completion coming very soon = B

- B – 1   Due date is very soon
- B – 2   Due date is soon

Daily Task Time Management: Completion is at some point in the near future=C

- C – 1   Task due date in the near future
- C – 2   Project due date in the future

If not completed, eventually Bs move to A's, C's move to B's. Let's look at a daily example.

Daily Task Schedule Example

A – 1   Email/Inbox

A – 2   Project Team Update

A – 3   Final Prep for 1 pm meeting

A – 4   Complete Weekly Update Report

A – 5   Work on Spread Sheet (75% complete) – Due in two days

A – 6   TBD as needed

A – 7   Set next Day Priorities

A – 8   Did we move toward Vision Achievement today?

B – 1   Complete or schedule any follow-up from 1pm meeting

B – 2   Prep for Thursday meeting

B – 3   Work on presentation to assign SMART Goal A.1-5 to Project Team B (50% complete due in 5 days)

C – 1   Work on Project Team C Training Manual (25% complete due in 3 weeks)

C – 2   Moved from P – 1, watch required 40-minute work video, due in 3 weeks

P – 1   Complete UDEMY Course on Vision Marksmanship®

P – 2   Read, Study Vision Marksmanship® Book

Vision Update Communication

Leadership will need to develop the means to communicate regular updates to the organization as a whole on the progression toward the Vision. Such updates are important so that the project teams and the organization as a whole is reminded how exactly the project they are completing aids in the overall Vision Achievement. It is very helpful to show this progress in graphic means. Such updates will help keep the project teams and individuals motivated toward the end goal.

This graphic shows a very simplified example. The Leadership may want to break this into the SMART GOALS for each Phase.

Vision Marksmanship

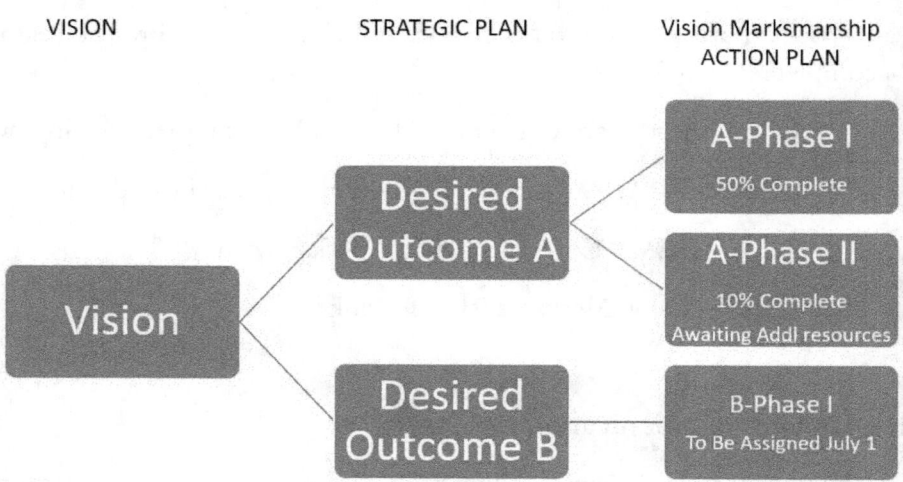

SECTION 8 – TEAM CARE

Change Creates

- Stress
- Risk
- Gain or Loss

Preparation and Training

- Provide necessary training, personnel are well trained!
- Equipped/Tools/ Resources
- Prepared for Success

Priorities

- Supervisor and team members align personal and professional priorities with organization and team priorities for duration of the project.

Future Focus

- Prepare the Team for the future
- Succession Planning/Professional Development

Responsibility

- Leader gives credit to the Team when the Team Succeeds
- Leader takes responsibility when the team fails
- Leader enforces policy and rules
- Leader provides course correction or performance improvement counseling
- Leader moves organization Mission and Vison forward through action

Project and Team Stress

- Monitor Team Members for conflict, being overwhelmed, stress
- Evaluate means to reduce stress
- Provide stress relief opportunities

Set Team up for Success

- Clearly communicate expectations
- Prepare the Team for success
- Give the team the resources and tools needed for success
- Give the necessary budget for success
- Provide the time needed for success
- Reward Benchmark achievements

SECTION 9 – SUMMARY

PUTTING IT ALL TOGETHER

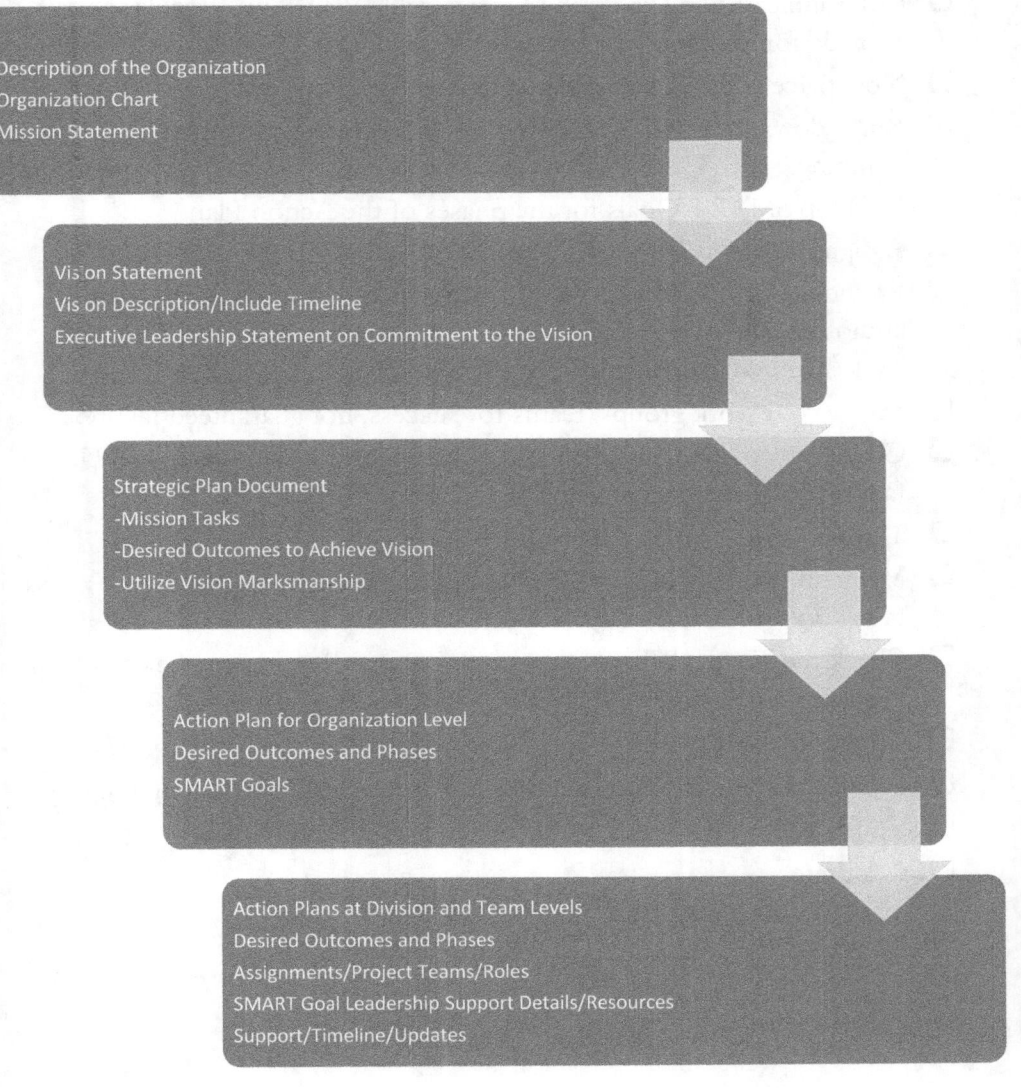

- Description of the Organization
- Organization Chart
- Mission Statement

- Vision Statement
- Vision Description/Include Timeline
- Executive Leadership Statement on Commitment to the Vision

- Strategic Plan Document
  - Mission Tasks
  - Desired Outcomes to Achieve Vision
  - Utilize Vision Marksmanship

- Action Plan for Organization Level
- Desired Outcomes and Phases
- SMART Goals

- Action Plans at Division and Team Levels
- Desired Outcomes and Phases
- Assignments/Project Teams/Roles
- SMART Goal Leadership Support Details/Resources
- Support/Timeline/Updates

Vision Marksmanship

- ☐ Develop the Vision, provide a Vision Statement that paints a picture of that Vision.
- ☐ Ensure that the Vision is in alignment.
- ☐ You now have your Target!
- ☐ Communicate and Clarify the Vision and MVGVP on a regular basis. Provide for updates.
- ☐ Now place your Organization in line with the target.
- ☐ Break down achieving the Vision by using Strategic Planning and Action Planning.
- ☐ Develop SMART Goals for the phases of the Action Plan.
- ☐ Assign the SMART Goals.
- ☐ Provide guidance, resources. Provide as decision-making model and authority levels for such decisions. Provide Training. Train ABCs of Task/Time Management.
- ☐ Set up your work groups/teams for success, not guaranteed failure.
- ☐ Guide or provide Course corrections, but do not micro-manage. Utilize failures for redirection/course correction.
- ☐ Team Care
- ☐ Maintain the daily Mission, but do not allow the Mission to cause a loss of focus on the Vision.
- ☐ Check the Target. Where is the organization? Provide course correction if needed.
- ☐ Communicate progress!
- ☐ Provide recognition and celebrate the accomplishments along the way.
- ☐ You have hit the Target! Enjoy the end result, the Vision.
- ☐ Celebrate

Start over, time for a new Vision.

About the Author

Steven Mitchell is the Managing Member of Vistane Group LLC which operates Vistane Group Consulting and Vistane Group Leadership Coaching. He has 40 years of experience in the Public and Private Sectors. Mitchell has been providing mentorship and organization assistance for over 20 years, and first developed the format for what would become Vision Marksmanship® in 2003. As a City Department Director for 16 years, he would use the Vision Marksmanship® system successfully for strategic planning and action planning. In consulting roles, Mitchell has used the system to assist organizations and mentored individuals in developing and moving toward a particular Vision. This has included everything from organization and project planning to individual career planning and coaching.

Thank You

I would like to thank my wife, children, daughters-in-law and grandchildren for their patience and assistance as I put together this great educational piece. I also thank my mentors over the years and am happy I can do the same for others. After developing this system many years ago, I now hope this updated easy-to-follow process will help others advance their individual and organizational Visions just as it has for me.

Steven P. Mitchell

www.ingramcontent.com/pod-product-compliance
Lightning Source LLC
Chambersburg PA
CBHW050313220526
45465CB00005B/1969